AF316773

Intertwined

Intertwined

A Poetry Collection

Dina Al Kabani

RESOURCE *Publications* · Eugene, Oregon

INTERTWINED
A Poetry Collection

Resource Publications
An Imprint of Wipf and Stock Publishers
199 W. 8th Ave., Suite 3
Eugene, OR 97401

www.wipfandstock.com

PAPERBACK ISBN: 979-8-3852-2896-6
HARDCOVER ISBN: 979-8-3852-2897-3
EBOOK ISBN: 979-8-3852-2898-0

VERSION NUMBER 08/01/24

Contents

Part One

Intertwined

Section One

Rebirth

Thread

The thread we strive to keep holding to
Stains red like the bond our fates sew
The feelings we cannot cast nor pass
Become the only petal our rose has

Back to back
We are caught in the same snare
That our lies captures
Side by side
We are parted by a mutual stare
That out truth ruptures
Our souls have long crossed paths
But the loneliness we hold dear
Flames this emptiness and sears
The fears crossing our bodies
That by our lives are muddied

***

Light walking through fractured glass
Scatters weak and broken
Injured by shattered rays reviving no grass
Abandoned thoughts awaken

The thread we no longer can hold to
Weakens as our fate is shaken
By the forbidden farewell you bid
A bond where you cannot undo what you did

***

Say not by tomorrow these connected hands are impossible
Say it Only when that day's arrival into our lives is plausible

***

The thread we strive to keep holding to
Stains red like the bond our fates sew
Forget not the cruelty from which it grows
We no longer live for the kindness it claws

When there is anything left of this world to eye
Let it only be this ragged red—soaked thread
Weaving a forbidden farewell like a setting sky
Tearing from this crimson an even deeper red

*****

The land of Night

Right now I breathe from the air you exhale
Losing the flow of time, I let my dreams sail
To the land of night . . .

****

You believe I exist holding dearly to being cruel
It is alright, for you I will keep playing the fool
You can only recognize my shattered pieces
Gathered by the brutality your heart releases

Do not lean your head on my chest
So cold for the warmness you nest
Slowly seizing it . . . slowly freezing it . . .
By the dead . . colored red . . . hatred of mine

The doors to the land of darkness alluringly open
From the triviality of this world my eyes are woken
Run hurt child . . . free and wild . . .
These doors will unfold every time you wish
For the land of night!

****

I passed down my nonexistence to you in the will I wrote
Leaving you with the regret your persistence has brought

You live by opening me, wound after wound
My torment and your salvation are tuned
Easily spoken . . . easily stolen . . .
By the transient . . . never meant . . . bless we taint

The doors open in the corners of our mind
A darkened land in every memory we cast behind
Faster than a flash . . . our lives dash . . .
Held wishes mattering nothing in either worlds

I still find myself anchored to this place
Twisted pain enjoying your frustrated face
Every night and day . . . every passing ray . . .
Becomes the prayer for our separation I made
In the land of night!

*****

Briar

Oh, fields of green
Never yearned for in your speech
A briar never seen
Will not bloom to your beseech

＊

Peace wishing, a broken music box
Plays a final melody in silence
I sing along words trying to coax
The rhythm of pain and violence

A revealed mirror reflects your soul
A sealed mirror sustains my call
Broken glass weaves your kindness and cruelty whole

Rest, rest in the depth of a dictated oblivion
Crave no more the briar you can only rave
Until the day of our never decreed reunion
I will become the rose soothing your grave

With my thorns, I will soothe your grave

＊

Distant fields of green, far beyond your reach
Bloom out of the joy of your torment
Do you wish for a briar or two, then tell me which
I will bloom it out of the tears you spent

＊

Longing, the music box keeps playing the melody
Gifting both of you your doom
Wordless song attunes your warmth to a memory
Echoing in your empty room

Do you still wish for that briar?
One pure desire
Will not raise you higher
Even if of wishing your heart never tires

***

I will embrace fire every night
So you will not have to go sleep alone
A moonless vault will be our light
Your cries of pain, the lullaby I own

Rest, rest in the depth of a dictated oblivion
Only there flutter the wings of freedom
Fear not the fate denying our reunion
My prayers create the equals kingdom

*****

Section Two

Entreat

Alluring Moon

Do not be afraid, tell all of your secrets to the night moon
Your perverse thoughts become the awakening crows croon

Streaming a light of ivory
Like an absolute tyranny
Dominates every angle of our sight
Creating a warm reverie
Veiling a twisted destiny
Defying cries draw to our might

Will the dawn come at last
Risen on our craving's mast?
The night still draws
My vision that goes
Holding the dusk irony so close

Your lies warm my smiles
Every falsity takes me miles
To a distant world
Where all we hold
Are the tears pain no longer defiles

***

Your soul stands naked before the night's mirror alone
Reflected by a shrouded silver of a moon trying to atone

A toneless chord
A petty reward
Devises severity into the night to infuse

A lifeless aim
A ceaseless blame
Wild imagination, hurt, runs loose

Will the night grant us a dream
In shreds of a thousand beams?
My wish still allures
These thoughts of yours
To join reality and fuse

These lies my heart can only protect
Whenever the wandering rain collects
The wounds we bear
Flowering the despair
Left for lustful leers to reflect

***

Your lies created for us a masterpiece
So do not let them for a single word cease

***

Will the dawn come at last
Risen on our craving's mast?
The night still draws
My vision that goes
Holding the dusk irony so close

Your lies warm my smiles
Every falsity takes me miles
My wishes for you
Prove only true
Upon a darkened moon we rile

*****

Leave Me Forgotten

My vision has always been in this cage of fear caught
To open my eyes and see you only in a passing thought

Afraid, I only hear the voice of my memories in lament
Transient instances yet leaving the river of time bent

I sought this solitude . . . I bought its fortitude
Left alone drowning in my past I was saved
I have turned my heart . . . into a delusive art
The love you found is a dream you merely raved

***

If I have to depend on someone, only this fear I can trust
So I will not hear your voice no more than a passing gust

Afraid, my dreams have nothing dazzling to seek
Protecting themselves with a pain that does not speak

A melody without a key . . . a horizon without a sea
I am content being buried in some forgotten document
Without a spell of magic, without a portraying classic
My seared petals are fragrant with eternity's scent . . .

***

My existence is folded in the cruelty of the cage
And there I kept you away from a maddening rage
Use it not to protect me, and turn no new page

***

I will not reach the light . . . no matter how long I fight
My emergence is gained by a double edged sword
Leave me on a dusty shelf, shed no notice to be lit
My piece into this world puzzle was never fit

Please do not . . .
Give me a notice I can proudly call a loss
Give my memory to a bond defining us

*****

Shadow

Every time I say I will become strong and start over again
The future never comes together and the past pieces remain
Telling me the perfect place is the spectators seats
There, weave fantasies warming the cold streets

When the time comes . . .
I will say everything to these fake days
Though I for then saved my love to say
But why if everything just floats away?

***

These fragments of memories had a meaning at their time
Treasured back then, now replayed by days again
I shove them in despite never wanting their pain

The heavenly rain my reaching fingers try to taste
Dyes every and each person forgetting me in its haste

You only see me when standing beneath a street light
A reflected shadow can only flutter beneath its bright

***

Let me shed tears, they ensure I can still feel
I made small scratches yet they are for real

***

I measure people's flaws and duplicity
To find them frighteningly brief and fleeting
Repeated mistakes forgotten with every new meeting

Words that only echo in my heart
Yet the deaf world gives them a price
The only gift it never fails to impart
Lives pendent on how it turns the dice

You recall seeing someone on a certain seat
You recall upon passing her your heartbeat
You laugh how you imagined and feel sorry
But even so, this remains our secret story

*****

Section Three

Snare

Hurry

That is why hurry, say it all, no need to pretend
The time to softly whisper is soon going to end

Explained by an unreasonable reason
Illustrated through a faithful treason
Right and wrong both lead astray

There is a place this rounded world does not turn to
Where I can kiss you and always call you dear
A corner in our mind where nothing we care to rue
Where aspirations and actuality become sheer

***

That is why hurry, say it all, the words you shun
The time for regrets coming is soon never to run

Two hands our regrets brief and represent
Keep running forward despite the present
Backward and forward both lead to no way

There is a place this rounded world does not turn to
Where destinations are not limited by its range
A corner in our mind where nothing we care to rue
Where time does not need to pretend to change

***

That is why hurry, do it now, no need to wait
Fulfillment will come but by the will of fate

My wish or yours, something will happen
Favored whether spoken or kept within
Words and actions both act the same play

There is a place unreachable hidden inside my heart
Where we need not push our steps in hurry
A wreck that blooms when this world falls apart
Shattered fragments our duality no longer carry

*****

Lines of Deceit

Why chase a happiness that only twists the days to come
While pain lays the way clearly ahead in a known strum?

I do not need to gaze at a beautiful scenery and ponder
To unveil the purpose and the wisdom laying under

By a simple stare you think
You can open my pages and read
But my eyes are a quite difficult to conceive book
The core of pain you want
To reach and desperately need
Is not a line you can perceive through a single look
It roots beyond what you can grasp . . .

***

Why wear a pride deeming graciousness lie—jaded
While simple truth frees our souls, gloriously naked?

I do not have to reflect at a sky, tranquil and serene
With my beauty I possess contentment to self—feign

The heart you seek to reveal
Is a searing burned passion
A fleet happiness or a pain always lingering to our lashes?
Slow down the rhythm
Let us love in a wavering old fashion
Until these feelings dye a meaning to our grateful ashes
They root beyond what any can grasp . . .

***

You read one line but find a hundred meanings
If I do not mislead you in my heart's maze
How else can I justify your curious gaze?

***

I want to hide just one real meaning between my words
That tells you I am not entirely empty inside
But touching this truth, even if written on solid boards
It shatters slowly into every moment we lied

I dress my words in wiles, deception that never allows
Our hearts to become bonded by pretentious vows
That root where we can grasp . . .

Let our hearts dance to my emptiness, madly growing
Doubled and tripled meanings to these words drawing

Godly Sage

Do not make me a golden calf you can worship
Be content with a mere sage you can simply revere
You will still savor heavens' taste from my lip
I invite you to a transgression with a retribution not severe

Your desire steps beyond any dream's boundary
Ill devotion you found
Into a yielding sound . . . heretic!

Without shame you turn every whim into a prayer
Without hesitation you speak a mind I cannot tame
I listen refuting your proofs I am the main player
In this reversed seats and flipped beats game

But when you look at me with these eyes and entreat
Fill the wine into this tie
Make your heart my . . . Olympus!

Raise it, raise it
Let your voice be hoarsened with my tribute
Raze it, raze it
The sorrow that you to my denial attribute
Fear me, fear me
Unless desperate, dare not come near me
Tear me, tear me
May pain lead me to the desire lost in me

***

Do not presume me of the gods you need to implore
Simply tell with humbleness your prayer
Raising me to their status I will hear you no more
To the end, the one and only payer

The cross I bear keeps growing heavy
Will any of this suffering fruit?
Let this sole question loot . . . Your life!

Miracle, miracle
Who could tell I will be to your crown the king
Cynical, cynical
I am the god to those who believe in nothing
Oracle, oracle
Foretells a serenity to your lust, metaphorical
Semi, semi-
Bless we found without knowing alchemy

***

I am a god who does not from high her gifts bestow
Struggle not to reach me, I am down this hell below

***

Cannot you see?
I am a lonely god seeking company
Provoke my acceptance with a look more than any other
Feel me, feel me
Abstaining in awe because I turn shame into honey
Seal me, seal me
I will still grant any wish unlike my cruel mother

Raise it, raise it
To the empire you gift me, be my Remus
Praise it, praise it
The miracle drawing my Jupiter to your Venus
Fear me, fear me
Unless desperate, dare not come near me

Break me, break me
May I find the desire that makes me

****

27

Section Four

Chase

Black Bird

No one looks at a sky that is grey
Though this muddy earth lives and preys
Every time its shady colors tearfully pray

Wishing to protect at least one thing
A bird hid the colors of his remaining wing
Into the depth of the grey
Where his dear wishes lay
Where can he now, like this, fly to
Shrouding with safety all what he had held to?

These eyes lingering over new horizons
Destined to a darkened vision one day
Though pain along suffering stays
By your side, I keep seeking a new ray

Infinitely embracing every reaching hand
It is enough for me if my fingertips land
Certain and safe, falling against yours
While a damned serenity our mind tours

***

Unafraid, having nothing left to be taken
Leaving the colors of his wing forsaken
In the depth of the grey
Waiting no false May
Where should he now head forward
Denied to sing one truthful word?

Endlessly, feathers of the fallings float
Dancing to the warmness of a haven
Lightened by a deceit, freed to board the boat
Of freedom steered by their jailor raven

***

Give me something you did not have to pay for
Give me back the heart I once for your sake bore
The wings that have no cutter
Are the ones that do not flutter
Telling the wind " never blow my way . . ."

***

I will not gift you a sky where you can fly
A mirror to an earth without any road
Along your side, the taste of a petty try
Frees our souls, no longer by anyone owed

Watering open skies with a hopeful cry
Weighing down the wandering feathers
The heart that for your sake turned dry
Blissfully at your fluttering, withers

*****

Wish

Darkness is everything you can see
Yet you stare right at me with it
Dimness you use to look through me
You know nothing there need to be lit

You cannot accept anyone at your side
Is your loneliness a burden I have to bide?

" I wish for your love "
Words that will not reach my heart
" I wish for your love "
No matter how many times you repeat
Its echoes remain frighteningly fleet

***

If love is all about pain
Then I have myself with whom this I share
To be alone is sometimes the only thing sane
Whether you are obliged to or deem it unfair

You do not have a single dream you wish to see
Why do you want to share this with me?

"I want to be your love "
Words I can never hear
"I want to be your love "
Turn this sole wish into hate
Maybe then we will be joined by fate

" I wish for your love "
Words that will not reach my heart
" I wish for your love "
It is not like every wish will just come true
Letting you wish is the only thing I can gift you

To the End of Time

The kiss you wake me with
Leaves no trace like a dispersed drop
The hug you warm me with
Cannot make seeping wounds stop

To whom are these thoughts wandering the space?
To whom are these gazes softening your face?
My heart can only follow after one rhyme
The chimes of the past, to the end of time . . .

***

Nothing can brighten eyes that clearly see the truth
No one can invite kindness dedicated just to soothe

Your mistakes draw a straight constant line
Your mending colors it with the pain of mine
The never ceasing trials turn into a single repeated loop
Taking our places in the light and shadow, trying to cope

***

I see myself reflected in your eyes
Your wakefulness is where my being lies
Wishing for tomorrow, I long to be gazed upon
As my entity disperses by fears of dying alone

***

What are these thoughts wandering for?
What do these gazes, softening, harbor?
Our hearts can only follow one rhyme
Each other's beats, to the end of time

*****

Section Five

Dye

Hallucination

The falling rain shatters the night's image
The moon glitters like a lonely broken gem
It pours paying an anger—seeping homage
Weaving the silence a tear—adorned hem

Like a parasite, the racing drops feed
On the silence of the night, choking it with sobs
Prayers slip down by a crying that never stops

Drop after drop, chasing, they create a stream
Washing off the dream lying within the dream
Flooding with destruction the womb of imagination
Closed eyelids impart their vision to a hallucination

How many times have you seen the same dream?

***

Envious darkness immerses the night's pieces
Easily the rain flows like your words through it
Crystallized by pain into a mosaic that ceases
The love and longing you feared to say and admit

The rain beading the night a necklace, turns it long
A time of regret, it accepts the gift and steals
The grace to flow smoothly, slowing my heart along

Dimness and sheerness perform their shared tricks
Decorating fresh flowers to a dead's tomb

Twisted dreams grown from hurt, nothing can fix
From a barren yet fertile bleeding womb

When was the last time you saw a dream?

***

Do not leave it a dream
Falling to a repeated scheme
Frightened to admit it exists
Let it madly incarnate
Rather than sublimely radiate
Invading when the reality mists

***

Drop after a drop, chasing, they create a stream
Trenched, beyond reach becomes that dream
Flooding with destruction the womb of imagination
A rebelling pain holds an overwhelming hallucination

Dimness and sheerness perform their shared tricks
Decorating fresh flowers to a dead's tomb
Twisted dreams grown from hurt, nothing can fix
From a barren yet fertile bleeding womb

Non—existing, who can deny that dream?

****

Red and Black

The star I hoped to guide my soul
No longer crowns the innocent role
The rhythm I let your words dance freely to
No longer blends with the play of being true

All the mirrors finally return clear
The curtains fall weighed down by fear

Black . . . shrouds my rack
The truth brings me back
To the wishes fear drew
Red . . . is how pain bled
Time stopped as I shed
Every touch I had with you

***

Your warm caresses slowly melted the ice
Ceasing the marigold I for cheated my dice
For the sake of your soul I dewed agony
Taste your salvation in a heavenly irony

Hopes kept holding desperately to " If fate may . . ."
Until no rehearsal was enough to recite this foul play

Black . . . shrouds every thought
Red . . . is what I wished and sought
These two no more remain two sides of the coin
The promise you selfishly made

Is no less than a brief shade
Where the loops of destruction and rebirth disjoin

***

Tenderness for once meant only frailly echoed
Hardened hearts where honesty is not bestowed
It is laughable how everything returns to its origin
Your solace left no trace on the deep wound within

Open your chest to one last cry
Tomorrow's rain shall leave no dye

Black holds the stage
Red breaks the cage
We move on this board to a final checkmate
Reward deceitfully calls
Punishment persistently befalls
The time for a mad blossom is never late

Black colors the past
Red replaces the past
Truth and lies now together hum
Love turns to a lie
Hatred recreates the tie
Pray that tomorrow never comes

*****

The Never Ending Rain

The shattered body I gathered its pieces with my breath
Now cuddles me, frail arms inviting to a dance of death
Hands too soaked in every taint
Cannot streak a blessed paint
Our whiteness is the blackness we seek of more
Our warmness is the hatred our hearts live for

Give me any name . . .
Not that I care having an identity
I exist in front of your eyes
Close them and I will not be

My gaze longs to your sight
Desiring no empty bright
They reflect in every action my existence right
Like lifting a rooted shadow to stand in the light

***

Passing transiently, nothing I wish to do for my sake
Memories are mere adornments to the soul they remake

Harbored so deep within is a wish needing to create
The perfect light only its true essence can animate
Us and let our hands move this cycle of fate

***

The never ending rain . . .
Seeping along unhealed wounds, judged by time
Tunes people's hearts into one sorrowful chime

The never ending rain . . .
Racing to the darkness of a barren land
Longing to caress a lonely reaching hand
The never ending rain . . .
Filling the emptiness your eyes reflect
Washing memories you failed to protect
The never ending rain . . .
Passing the hands you desperately raise
The undone mistakes, it will never erase

So, let these hands dye this never ending rain

*****

Section Six

Finale

Thank You

What are you doing now the one I am thinking of?
My thoughts of you are where they can freely love

What place did your wandering leave you in
Is it where only the days ahead occupy your mind?
Where you will not regret the words kept within
Can you only protect what is dear leaving it behind?

It was so easy for you to set on a journey
Yet I can still feel in each step your agony
Chasing nothing, your destination is clear
You escaped the swirl of pain, what is to fear?
Is it the scent of bless still calling you back
Knowing it only steals hopes, never gained aback?

How many times has my heart been ripped apart?
Yet I can always find the piece where you reside
I hold it amidst the hatred devouring my heart
Every time I put it, seeps the anguish I cannot hide
Torn, I am freed for a moment from its black hue
For tearing my heart overly, I say " thank you "

***

Even if I wish to, who am I to call for you
When pain is the only thing of me that is true?
A bird left without a single feather
Selfishly inviting you with her to wither

If I were to turn into a breeze and storm
I will probably destroy you within my rage too
My black heart sees the world in monochrome
For accepting to be tainted in it, I say " thank you "

***

What are you doing now, the one I am thinking of?
Do you mention my name every once and a while?
My thoughts of you are where they can freely love
Away from my heart so I can look at them and smile

In a faithless world, you showed me a feeling not hateful
Even if it is dyed in pain, for this loneliness I am grateful
Forgiving no one, including you, this I do not rue . . .
For accepting my blind malice, I say " thank you "

*****

Remember

A gentle voice sings about eternity
Deceiving life with a wished serenity

I wonder why was I given yet another try
Though meeting you did not undo any goodbye

I wonder if the past is something I wish to restore
As the circle of trust and hurt always fits our lives
A star, knowing how to follow, our expectations tore
So we would not shed tears when tomorrow arrives

Faraway . . . Faraway . . . with no words to say
I have entrusted my memories with an eternal silence
Forever . . . Forever . . . as long as we sever
Every bond, only this pain remains our alliance

Why . . . why do I find myself standing alone
In a world where everyone craves to atone?

The flowers I hold sear
The hours I spend shed tears
But I know you will always be here

When I finally lay to an eternal sleep
And suffering no longer matters to seep
The most painful, your memory, I will keep

Remember . . .

*****

Part Two

Thesis

Section One

Creation

Baptism of the Crimson Waves

The crimson waves whisper in my ears
A new heart beats
A dwelling darkness their piety sears
The born light meets
The line joining earth and heaven

The ancient ballad of miracles and wonders
Engenders an inherent wish, purity sunders
The flute of the day plays to the night's

The crimson waves in a baptism collide
Mantling the shore, the sky and the sea twining
Intermarrying life in the sea deep inside
Birthing a destined to end beginning

Connate sprouts dance to the ancient ballade
Consorted by praises, they open and flower
To instants of eternity the budding essence had

The crimson waves whisper in my ears
The birth song of love
The dwelling darkness their piety fears
Is left for mortals to rove

✶✶✶✶

Miracle

Oh, loving dear great father
Raising us above every other
Your wisdom cast us down
In this covenant we drown

***

The miracle of creation ended in six days
But the darkness we create paves endless ways

Your emptiness seeks a lost compassion
That can fill a broken tie
You turn away from me and imagine
My words a lustful lullaby

Do not chase the sky with your eyes
There is a whole world in mine to see
Always adore the secret which lies
In the depth of your heart
Which I humbly impart . . .
The secret you grew from my lap

***

Oh, loving dear great father
Raising us above every other
This pain to my womb you gift
A joint birth that neither will lift

***

The miracle from all dreams has been stolen
So we can leave our souls for adoration open

My emptiness seeks its other half
A passion that fills my incomplete part
So I can finally have a free laugh
That only resounds in my own heart

Being created of a sole white
Warped my being in a constant black
Always calling for the things I lack
Breaking that rib . . . I victoriously rip
The freedom of a soul longing to fight

***

We sit now to a familial banquet
Each tasting his unspoken regret
Longing we praise in an unholy mass
With these hands, not clerical nor physical
In the maze of our minds, I create a miracle

***

Oh, loving dear great father
Raising us above every other
Our survival was pendent on two
What is the essence of this soul's hue?

****

Meteor of the Outcast

The garment of heavens that cast me denuded
Ravels along my eyes at this resurrection I attend
The rags of my body no longer bless—hooded
Attest the light, a gift I am now able to rend

A reward to a covenant of servitude
This cold doubtful heart of solitude
A meteor rolls down birthing the flames of life

Wisdom devised into a twisted plan
Seeking purpose in the agony of man
Falling pawn the end scriptures ink and line
The time of the postponement promise
A trap or a path to the sought bless?
Humbled pawn to reflect every birthed soul sign

***

The conceit of self, emerging through impatience
Is brought down by a miracle of clay
Admiration to a servitude devoid of complaisance
Awakens to deny any other say

A display to a covenant of faith
These sins which pride bathes
A meteor rolls down paving the flames of reign

A potency devised into a twisted plan
Seeking execution in the agony of man
Falling pawn to justify the end scriptures

The time of the postponement promise
A trap to an exalted yet lost bless
Humbled pawn to regret over haughty strictures

A meteor rolls down . . .
The star of misfortune brings down the star of the dawn
Fueled by those chosen to feed over what is gone

*****

Sempiternity I

Given rise out of mud
Creation began ending by two
And by the will of god
You shall serve me and I will guide you

***

Plowing the sprouting earth
A man raised his hands in the presence of kings
Afraid loneliness will be his berth
He kneeled and prayed for his resonance to ring

"Here is a prayer you will hear for a reply
A peer inside your rib and core
But on our name you both will rely"
Then out of whiteness another soul soared

Hand in hand through the garden they walked
In the sweat of their hard work were soaked
Eyes longing for knowledge
Feet fearing the fatal edge

They were born in a garden of heaven
Lost it for a forbidden succession
Cast to a woe of endless regret
Remained none of the kindness when they first met

Given rise out of mud
Creation began ending by two

And by the holy union buds
The path of trials to live through

*****

61

Lullaby

Small hands, too frail to hold a shred of a dream
Reach weakly through what birthed tears deem
A lullaby . . .

The tears of heavens repeatedly flow and engulf
The earth my tears keep reviving every crook and gulf

The feel of a trailing soft touch
Leaving of warmness not much
Nursing it slowly from my breast
Here, weave yourself a small nest
From a lullaby . . .

***

Since your birth your eyes looked up at the skies
Wondering to where that lonely bird flies?
Since your growth your feet wandered around
And no satisfying answer could be found
In a lullaby . . .

***

A chant of glory
Tearful and sorry
Let mercy these praying raised hands meet
May you know nothing
Never unfold your wing
And this missing call of home never repeat

The dreams you took from my heart
A wale in me leave and impart
These nights of worried thought
Your journeying has brought
A single word no more can hold you in my arms
Yours embracing this world's endless charms

" Goodbye "

***

The truth of a lingering soft kiss
The psalm for your pain to hush
Embedding how much my tears miss
The warmth of your forehead, my bliss

The feel of a trailing soft touch
Leaving of warmness not much
Nurse it slowly from my breast
And weave yourself a small nest
From a lullaby . . .

Section Two

Wallowing

Song of Happiness

An old song lays you to sleep
A rhyme denies you were here
The promise you said you will keep
Will simply vanish unlike your tear

The touches you feel and leave behind
The gestures you receive and make
All these drizzles of memories aligned
Are born for nothingness to take

Gloria, what are you so afraid of?
What will it do looking up above?
Hollow and dark clouds
Overseeing your own being

Is not this darkness what your eyes are used to?
Only now do not your nights seem so true?
Yet this song of happiness you hear
Will not ever deceive your ears

***

Was not it here where you wished to play?
Where no one came and asked you to stay?
The sorrow you felt gave the joy
Brief breaths to make a new toy

You never needed play hide and seek
Your eyes, sullied, knew where to peek

And inside, slept a beautiful doll
Porcelain beauty, no one recalls

Gloria, whose these touches that feel so kind?
Just in this immortal darkness you can find
Songs of happiness that rise
And do not know how to tell lies

An old song, yet played just for you
Washing off your soul that violet hue
Only the scars you bear
Tell " someone stood there . . ."

*****

Tearful Pride

Tears dye every beginning of life
Yet you will not let them run down
Soaking your heart, pride is still rife
Always clutching to it like a clown

And smiles along grieve go on
Like a song nothing can interrupt
Dreams, seen by your eyes, turn wan
Only your happiness remains abrupt

This sky will give you rain and warmness
But it will always be there shading you
Tainted rain washes you without bless
Your fate has been dyed by its blue

***

Pain, scar so deep
Wounds, sprout and seep
Sorrows, heap . . . for guilt to reap

Pain, scar so deep
Wounds, sprout and seep
Sorrows, heap . . . still, the price is cheap

Your breaths revive every death you dealt
Your regrets pillage every passion you felt

Pain, scar so deep
Wounds, sprout and seep
With tears .

***

Racing sunsets call and derive
Tears that are cruel to shed
Having only loss to bring and revive
They sleep on a carnations bed

Goodbye . . . days gone by
Prayers would only taint the memory
A salute, formal and mute
Tears would only sully the reverie

This sky will give you rain and warmness
But it will always be there shading you
Tainted rain washes you without bless
You have taken for yourself its blue . . .

For eternity .

*****

Lacrimosa

Wait till the sky turns to a dark line
Then let the love you harbor shine

***

The me reflected in the water is gone
Since our days back in heaven
For our souls have always been one
Together, our sins became seven

Sleeping love that you keep
Give it all to your own soul
Selfish love, pure and deep
Draws your dignified fall

Lacrimosa befalls my heart
With regret it writes my name
And as my vision slowly departs
I realize it has always been the same

The glory that lifted you higher
Into the cold funeral pyre . . .
You witness it burn, the way days erase
The muddy existence you could not raise

Dreamy eyes abandoning hope cruelly awaken
By a crimson moon are embraced and taken
White and black wings, fly and entwine
Into the night where your love can shine

***

A flickering star, the night lone dancer
Fading, I entrust it with my tale
Knowing there will be no given answer
Is proudly gone without a howl or wail

This sky . . . is so high . . .
I cannot reach it with these hands
What of prayers that cannot fly?
From of a cruel mercy are banned

***

Into shattered dust, delusive and wretched
Is your life—paid, sin—worth glory
Along with your ashes, you watch it ended
Leaving no single echo of your story

Close your eyes and count to ten
The forgiveness that would only pen
Your faith to pain, if to my embrace lent
Will be given washed by my torment

***

Lacrimosa befalls my heart
With regret it writes my name
And as my vision slowly departs
I realize it has always been the same

My lips repeat a song
The simple wish to belong
The quiet prayer turns to a refrain
That heaven keeps for itself to sustain

Seeping eyes, cry and turn the world a crimson dye
Denied hearts wail " your fortune like your hearts, is a lie "
White and black wings, fly into one and entwine
Into the night where your love devours the skyline

*****

Section Three

Ending

Sempiternity II

Given rise out of mud
Creation began ending by two
And by the will of God
You shall serve me and I will guide you

***

Wandering the devoid earth
A man raised his hands in the presence of kings
Afraid darkness will be his berth
He kneeled and prayed for a pair of wings

" Here is a prayer you will not hear for a reply
You shall never be given ones
You will not look down tainting the purity to fly
By the greed that innately runs "

To the sins of the eldest I admit
Why punished for what I did not commit
Descending earth,
What can be left of my pride but humbleness?

" You were born in a garden of heaven
Lost it for a forbidden succession
You could learn from a black raven
But not to maintain the sacred haven "

Still denied, the man turned his back
On the holy light, heart drenched in black

Angered, the divine rage flooded and poured
" Let thy be judged by the justice sword "

***

Helplessly, the man lived only for his sake
Following what his soul called for
Futile profanations will not make mightiness shake
As it continued to proudly soar

Dust to dust . . .
He realized death is a must
From mud to mud, what else to satisfy but pleasure
Knowing it will be the only thing left to measure

" Just a pair of wings to feel that divine . . .
Light, how can I claim it to be mine?! "
But heavens knew what they have created
Obtaining a will, to defiance ill—fated

***

Consumed by existence, turning into apathy
A heart still cried alone and pained
At the wailings of purgatory tears of sympathy
Were shed three times when the sky rained

***

The quick to fade seed of regret . . .
This endless struggle is all you will get

***

Abandoned, could acknowledge no light
How to reach it at that height?
Abandoned, " Cursed thy dreams to wander
Dispelled by the divine spears of thunder "

A bond broken from the start
By the potency of authority, by the taste of will
Blessed submissiveness cannot fruit in a vivid heart
Waiting the apocalypse hopeless hands would fulfill

*****

76

Dies Irae

The sun lays with the moon
Fulfilling an old prophecy
The wind plays a song of wrath and mercy

The earth shatters to tumulus
Out of its essence awaken us
Created, livened and ended in a muss

Rise in fear and owe
Do not turn your face on me
You are yourself own foe
Let thy will alone be . . . your justice see . . .
Yours, to whom wine and blood are spilled alike

Damned by sin or blessed by belief
Today there is no escape
The day of judgment
Long destined, has come
Marred souls, melt into the one
Who took perfection's shape
The blaze of rebellion, the breeze of docility
Each I shall hold and sum

***

Hungry, fire leaves a third devoid of green
Roamed no more, a blue third is red's reign
Soaring light leads a third to a revival scene

***

Speechless, your senses speak
Of the just amends they seek
Of your sins, your flesh and skin reek

Rise in fear and owe
I will grow for you new wings
You are yourself own foe
Bequeath you no less than kings, with dominions rings
Yours, to whom praise and blasphemy fruits alike

Damned by sin or blessed by belief
Today there is no escape
The day of judgment
Long warned, has come
Marred souls, bow to the one
Who took perfection's shape
The blaze of rebellion, the breeze of docility
Each I will hold and sum

***

Tired, lights return to their essence
Truthfully now shine and bud
An enraged mother pining to punish
Those bearing not the seal of god
An ancient purity burdened gold
Washes those created of mud

***

Damned by sins
Never will you soar upon your demise
Blessed by belief
Never can you discern truth from lies

***

Damned by sin or blessed by belief
Today there is no escape
The day of judgment
Always present, now comes

Marred souls, listen to the one
Who took perfection's shape
The blaze of rebellion, the breeze of docility
Each I will hold and sum

Praises proclaim one to wear the rod and the bay
Built by who strayed, the ancient tablets sins weigh
Let mercy befall thee, if he may

*****

Requiem of the Crimson Waves

There . . . say . . . can you see?
There, beyond these distant parts
Lands that cannot be drawn on charts
My soul is a bird inside of me
Flipping with the crimson waves

Holding this vision
Engraved to my very core
I should not be afraid anymore

***

There . . . say . . . can you hear?
There, beyond the skies our cries clear
Songs played by the angels harps
My soul is a bird that sings and sharps
While reaching to the crimson waves

Singing this song
Engraved to my very core
I should not be afraid anymore

The crimson waves now collide
Broken on the rocks like glass
Dead in the sea, deep inside
Rising only to get broken, alas

***

The crimson waves whisper in my ears
A new heart beats

This endless rain becomes my tears
A reborn soul meets
The line joining earth and heavens

The ancient ballad of repose and storm
Engenders out of the chaos the world's form
The flute of the night plays to the day's

The crimson waves in a requiem collide
Mantling the shore with a guile sinning
Intermarrying death in the sea deep inside
Birthing a transient gauzy beginning
Rising to get broken, alas . . .

***

Soaked by a vision engraved to my core
I collect the fragments of my soul's ore
Worth naught when shattered by fears
Loneliness ordains their existence no more

***

The crimson waves whisper in my ears
An ancient song of love
This endless rain becomes my tears
Having my eyes to rove

Birds, souls of the lost, loud and sharp
Consort shy hums
Songs for pain by the angels' harp
Echo in doldrums
Earth no longer joins the heavens

My sorrows dance to the ancient ballad
Enchained by antithesis my being flowers
Instants of eternity my resting essence had
My born mortal soul with curiosity towers
Grasping the mourning crimson waves

*****

The End